HOW TO DRAW

POKéMON

SINNOH HEROES

Illustrated by Ron Zalme

ISBN-13: 978-0-545-10265-0
ISBN-10: 0-545-10265-0

12 11 10 9 8 7 6 5 4 3 2   8 9 10 11 12/0

Printed in the U.S.A.
First printing, September 2008

SCHOLASTIC INC.
New York Toronto London Auckland Sydney
Mexico City New Delhi Hong Kong Buenos Aires

A LAND OF POKÉMON MYTHS AND HEROES

Welcome to Sinnoh, a region of the Pokémon world that's home to many powerful Pokémon. Some are even the stuff of legends! Now these mighty Pokémon are gathered together in one place, with step-by-step instructions and tips on how to draw each of them. If you're ready to become a Pokémon sketch artist, then this is the book for you!

HOW TO USE THIS BOOK

You can go through the book in order or flip straight to your favorite Pokémon, but it's always a good idea to warm up first. Read below and practice drawing some of the Pokémon in the beginning of the book. Once you're comfortable with the basics, you'll be equipped to take on the likes of Dialga and Palkia!

TOOLS OF THE TRADE

You can draw Pokémon just about anywhere—all you need is a pencil, an eraser, and some paper! A pen or marker is good for tracing over your finished pencil lines. You may also want colored pencils, markers, or crayons to color in your drawings.

BASIC GUIDELINES

Every drawing in this book starts with a few simple guidelines. Draw them to the same size you want for your finished drawing, and remember to pencil them in lightly so you can easily erase them later. Before you start to draw a Pokémon, picture a line that extends from its head all the way down the middle of its back. That's your first guideline! Then add other guidelines to indicate arms or legs.

Your guidelines will also show how large your finished drawing will be.

TOOLS OF THE TRADE

No matter what shape a Pokémon may be, you can still draw it by putting together basic shapes like circles, rectangles, and triangles. In fact, just about any picture you see can be built from basic shapes! This book will show you how to go from basic shapes to a finished Pokémon drawing, but you don't have to stop there. To sharpen your skills, look at everyday objects around you and try breaking those down into their basic shapes, too.

GETTING AHEAD!

The two most important shapes in a Pokémon drawing are the head and the body. Notice how the oval for Azelf's head has two curved guidelines inside it? The vertical guideline runs down the center of the face, through the nose and mouth. The horizontal guideline is at the level of the eyes. Guidelines usually curve in the direction the Pokémon's head is facing.

Here, the guidelines show that Azelf is looking to the left.

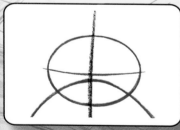

Draw straight guidelines when a Pokémon is facing forward, like this Lickilicky!

Don't worry if it still takes you a few tries to get your Pokémon perfect. Even professional artists need to practice—and the more you practice, the better you'll get!

THINK YOU'VE GOT ALL THAT? THEN IT'S TIME TO DRAW THE FIRST POKÉMON!

LICKILICKY

Just as its name suggests, this pink, plump Pokémon has a super-long tongue. Lickilicky can use this tongue to grab objects or even use it to battle opponents— look out for its Lick attack! This Lickilicky here looks pretty friendly, but if you try to befriend it, you might want to bring a towel along. Get too close to a Lickilicky and you could end up covered in its drool!

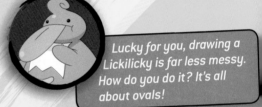

Lucky for you, drawing a Lickilicky is far less messy. How do you do it? It's all about ovals!

2 Using your guidelines from Step 1, add features like Lickilicky's arms, legs, and tail. Its face has round little eyes and a wide, beaming mouth. Don't forget the curlicue on the top of its head!

1 Start with some guidelines. Because Lickilicky's body is so stout, both guidelines are almost the same size. Next, add an oval for its head and a big, egg-shaped oval for its body.

3 Now that you have Lickilicky's body drawn, you're ready to add details like Lickilicky's markings. Notice how those three stripes on its belly curve upward a little—that gives Lickilicky's belly a rounded, 3D effect.

4 Once you've finished the details, you can erase the guidelines and take a look at your drawing. This is your chance to make some changes until you're satisfied. When you're done, you're ready to trace your pencil lines and color.

5 You only need three colors for Lickilicky. It's almost entirely pink! The bib-shaped mark on its neck is white, and so are its claws. That just leaves yellow for the stripes on its belly.

Try drawing Lickilicky with its tongue out. Is it trying to grab something tasty to eat?

1 You'll start with three guidelines for Gallade, but it's easier than it looks. Start with one long line for Gallade's body, then lines for its arms and legs. Draw a circle for Gallade's head and an oval for its waist, but keep the rest of your shapes long and lean.

2 Fill in the lines for Gallade's limbs and body, then add the features on its head and cheeks. Take a close look at this step: notice how the tips of its forearms are curved just a little to make them more elegant.

GALLADE

Gallade is a master of swordsmanship, but you'll never see it carry a weapon. Gallade doesn't need one: this honorable Psychic-and-Fighting-type Pokémon can battle with the blades that extend from its elbows! Both Gallade and Gardevoir evolve from Kirlia, a Psychic-type Pokémon, but Gallade will only evolve from male Kirlia.

How do you capture Gallade's dashing spirit? Don't be afraid to exaggerate your guidelines here— Gallade looks best when striking a dramatic pose!

3 This is the detail step! Add lines to Gallade's head, hands, and feet, and don't forget to draw in its eye. The fin on its chest is easier to draw than it looks. To figure out where to draw the lines, imagine a half circle overlapping its body.

Here's an idea: try drawing Gallade in other action poses! How about two Gallade getting ready to demonstrate their dueling skills?

4 After you erase your guidelines, an intense Gallade should be looking back at you. Now's the time to adjust any final details—make sure you're satisfied before moving on to color.

5 Battling against Gallade is hard, but coloring it is easy! Its head and upper body are green, with a blue-green fin. Gallade's lower body and cheeks are white, and its details are pink!

MANAPHY

Why is Manaphy known as the Migration Pokémon? Perhaps it's because Manaphy will travel great distances to return to the seafloor where it was hatched. Manaphy may be small—it's only a foot tall—but this Water-type Pokémon could swim across an ocean!

A big head and large eyes are features associated with cuteness, and Manaphy is no exception! The circle for Manaphy's head should be larger than the triangle shape for its body.

1 Manaphy is leaping in delight, so curve the guideline for its body and use a V-shaped guideline for its arms. Add the circle for its head and then a triangle for its body. Don't forget a curvy line for Manaphy's antenna!

2 Curve the tips of triangle to make Manaphy's feet. When you add its arms, remember that Manaphy's arms are longer than its body. Fill in the lines for its antennae, and add some ovals for its eyes and the markings on its face.

3 You're not done with ovals yet! Use ovals for the details of Manaphy's eyes and the marks on its belly.

4 You know what to do by now—erase the guidelines and look at your artwork! How does your Manaphy look to you?

How do you think Manaphy's antennae would look if it was feeling surprised? Sleepy? Excited?

5 *Manaphy is as blue as the seas it inhabits. Just add some yellow and red for its colorful markings and pink for its mouth. See the way the red mark on its belly gleams like a gem? To give it a shiny highlight, leave a small white oval area when you color it in.*

You can convey a Pokémon's emotion in the way you draw its entire body. Try drawing Manaphy in different moods!

THREE HIDDEN LEGENDS

Sinnoh's lakes may be hiding a powerful secret! This region is home to a trio of Legendary Pokémon: Uxie, Mesprit, and Azelf. All three are hard to spot, but you may find them if you know where to look underwater . . .

1 Put in your guidelines. As you add the oval for Uxie's head and a teardrop shape for its body, notice how Uxie's body and tail form the shape of a backwards J.

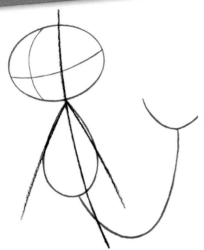

2 When you draw Uxie's body, there are two points to remember. First, you can use a quick circle for the outer shape of Uxie's head. Second, don't forget to add that extra line to the lowest curve of Uxie's tail.

UXIE

Is this mysterious Pokémon sleeping? Not at all! Uxie's eyes are closed even when it's awake—and that may be a good thing. Legend says that it has the power to wipe the memory of those who see its eyes! But Uxie also has the power to transmit information to people, so it's known in Sinnoh as the Being of Knowledge.

If you keep practicing, you'll be able to draw Pokémon from memory! Do you remember how to draw Manaphy? The proportions for Uxie's body are like Manaphy's: a cute, large head and a small body.

3 Just a few more details to go! Add Uxie's eyelids, mouth, and the lines on its head. You're not done with its tail yet—add some triangles and gem-like details.

4 Hmm... is that a thoughtful Uxie you see when you erase your guidelines? Now's the time to adjust your details!

5 Color Uxie's body a soft gray, and make its eyes and the top of its head yellow. Just like Manaphy, you can make the red details shine like jewels if you add a little white highlight.

Sometimes you want to change something in your drawing, but you don't know where to start.

There are some little tricks to help get you unstuck: try a change in your perspective. Look at your picture from a distance or hold it up to a mirror. Don't have a mirror? You can just flip over the paper and hold it up to the light!

AZELF

In Sinnoh, legends say that Azelf originated from the same egg as Uxie and Mesprit. Azelf is known to the people of Sinnoh as the Being of Willpower—perhaps it can grant people the drive to accomplish great things! You'll need some willpower and determination of your own to find out, because Azelf can be hard to find. It usually sleeps deep beneath a lake, but even while it sleeps, it helps to keep the world in balance!

1 This Azelf is flying gracefully through the air, so make your first guideline one big swoop. Use ovals for the shape of Azelf's head and body.

2 Now it's time to sketch in the lines of Azelf's body and tail. Make sure they flow together! Because Azelf is looking up, you'll want to draw its eyes closer to the top of its head.

3 Now you can move on to the finishing details, like Azelf's eyes, mouth, and the decorations on its tail.

4 Does your Azelf look like it's taking flight? Stick with your drawing and don't give up—sometimes, little changes make all the difference!

5 Azelf is light gray, with a blue face and curious, bright yellow eyes. Don't forget to put in the highlights on its tail!

Has anyone ever seen Azelf together with Uxie and Mesprit? You have—all you have to do is draw all three of them together in a group picture!

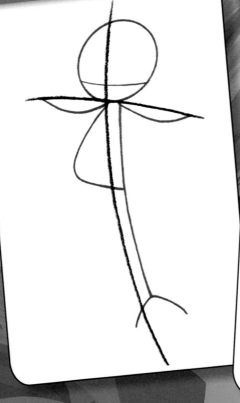

MESPRIT

The people of Sinnoh call Mesprit the Being of Emotion, and the stories say it was able to teach people about both sorrow and joy. Like Uxie and Azelf, Mesprit normally sleeps at the bottom of a lake. That doesn't mean it has to miss out on what happens on the surface, though—Mesprit can send its spirit soaring!

3 Now you can fill in Mesprit's other details. Mesprit's expression should be a little playful, or even mischievous!

5 Like Uxie and Azelf, Mesprit's body is light gray. Don't forget to make its eyelids gray, too! The rest of its head is pink.

4 Erase your guidelines and take a good look at your artwork. If your Being of Emotion isn't just right, don't get upset! It can take several tries to get a drawing the way you want it.

This Mesprit is staying still, but why not picture it soaring over a lake? Look back at Azelf for ideas about how to shape this new pose!

THE THIRD TIME'S THE CHARM

Each Trainer in the Sinnoh region starts their journey with one of three Pokémon: Turtwig, Chimchar, or Piplup. These Pokémon might be small and cute to begin with, but once they evolve . . . and then evolve again . . . they become a trio of Pokémon big and tough enough to take on any opponent!

EMPOLEON

Empoleon is the fully evolved form of proud little Piplup! Piplup evolves into Prinplup, a Pokémon whose wings are powerful enough to snap trees. But once Prinplup evolves into Empoleon, look out! This Water-and-Steel-type Pokémon stands over five feet tall and can use the sharp edges on its wings to slice through ice floes. What's more, it can swim as fast as a motorboat!

1 Start your drawing with a solid base—Empoleon's body is one tall triangle. Two long leaf shapes form Empoleon's wings. How long? They should reach almost all the way down to Empoleon's feet, which are drawn from two more triangles.

2 Block in Empoleon's legs, its three horns, and its V-shaped collar. Don't forget the triangular edges on its wings!

3 There are a lot of details to add in Step 3, but it all comes down to triangles again! From the spikes on the inside of Empoleon's wing to the jagged markings on its forehead, you can do just about everything in this step by breaking the features down into triangular shapes.

Those three horns on Empoleon's head aren't just for show. In a group of Empoleon, the leader will have the longest horns. See if you can draw a small group of Empoleon and their fearless leader!

4 Are you finished? Erase your guidelines and take another look. Did you get all the details? There are a lot of them, so don't feel bad if you missed some!

5 Empoleon's body is black with regal blue highlights. Don't forget the yellow claws, feet, and horns!

Empoleon looks imposing, but the key to drawing it is easy: it's all about triangles!

1 Once you have your basic guidelines, use triangles to outline the shape of Infernape's bent legs. See how one triangle is larger? That's because Infernape's left foot is further forward.

2 Now flesh out Infernape's body and limbs. Add ovals to its head, knees, and the back of its hands. Use round shapes to add all its toes—there are five on each foot.

You'll use a lot of ovals when drawing Infernape. Even the inside and outside of this Pokémon's ears are shaped like narrow ovals.

INFERNAPE

Infernape, a Fire-and-Fighting-type Pokémon, is the final evolution of Chimchar. It should be no surprise that this Infernape looks ready for action: Infernape has mastered its own special form of martial arts. This Pokémon's spirit burns as fiercely at the flames on its body. And when things get tough, Infernape's Ability, Blaze, can power up its fiery moves.

3 Time to fill in the details. That includes adding more ovals for the inside of Infernape's ears and the details on its shoulders, chest, hands, and knees! Don't forget to use jagged lines for the fur on its arms, legs, and torso.

4 Erase your guidelines and touch up any details you need to fix. Then pat yourself on the back. You've just drawn an intense Infernape!

5 Infernape's fur is brown with white highlights and blue and gold details. For its flame, use a fiery mix of reds and yellows!

What's next for Infernape? You've drawn Infernape crouched in a fighting stance and ready for battle, now draw Infernape unleashing its martial arts moves!

TORTERRA

Torterra, a Grass-and-Ground-type Pokémon, evolves from Grotle, the evolved form of Turtwig. Standing over seven feet tall and weighing over half a ton, Torterra's strengths are power and toughness rather than speed. In fact, sometimes it must seem to be moving very slowly—or not at all—because small Pokémon have been known to try nesting on its back! When a herd of Torterra is migrating, it looks like an entire forest is on the move!

1 Let's start with those guidelines: one long line for Torterra's body, and a shorter line to show where its legs start. Then add a big oval for Torterra's carapace. The small oval touching it is the leafy tree growing from Torterra's back.

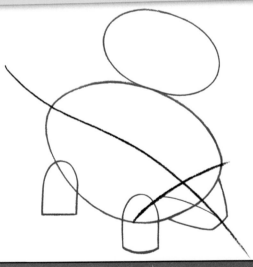

2 Flesh out your guidelines with some triangles. Add Torterra's tail and the spikes on its shell and head. Don't forget a second oval for the tree on its back.

Torterra's body structure is different than the Pokémon you've seen so far, but the hardest part is the level of detail on Torterra's back. The rest is simple!

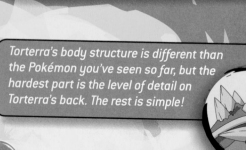

3 It's all in the details! Give Torterra's carapace some texture: use wiggly lines to turn ovals into the leaves of a tree and add greenery to the base of Torterra's spikes. To make the spikes and the tree look 3D, add small lines for the bark and the edges of the spikes.

4 Almost done! Erase the guidelines and see how Torterra looks.

5 It's only appropriate that a Grass-and-Ground-type like Torterra be mostly green and brown. Use an earthy brown for its legs, belly, and (of course!) the trunk of the tree. Experiment with mixing different greens on Torterra's carapace to make it look like it's really green and alive.

What kind of Pokémon might nest on Torterra's back? Use your imagination and try sketching a Torterra with some new Pokémon friends.

21

POWERED-UP POKÉMON!

Magby evolves into Magmar, and Elekid evolves into Electabuzz. Those Pokémon have already been spotted in other regions, but this is your opportunity to study their final evolutions up close. Let's take a look at Magmortar and Electivire!

Magmortar has lots of details and a new pose, but don't worry, you're ready to take the heat. Look again and you'll see that Magmortar is drawn from lots of circles and ovals. You can definitely do this!

1 As always, put down your guidelines first. For Magmortar's head and body, draw a small circle overlapping a much larger oval. Add another circle to form the end of Magmortar's extended arm.

2 Now you can put in circles for Magmortar's shoulders and ovals for its legs. Remember, Magmortar's shoulders start just below its head.

Here's a quick trick to help you draw the end of Magmortar's extended arm, and it's all done with—you guessed it—circles! See the circle you drew for the end of Magmortar's arm? Start at the left edge and draw a larger circle to represent the outer end of Magmortar's arm. Then draw a circle just inside that one.

MAGMORTAR

One look at Magmortar and you'll know it's a Fire-type. This Pokémon evolves from Magmar and likes things hot, hot, hot—Magmortar happily makes its home in volcanic craters. What's more, its arms can shoot flames of over 3,600 degrees Fahrenheit. That's hot enough to melt metal!

3 Add wiggly lines for the flames and markings on Magmortar's body. Don't forget the details—there are four spikes on Magmortar's back, but you can only see part of two of them.

4 Once you erase the guidelines, see how your Magmortar looks. Does it look like it's ready to rumble? If not, you can fix it!

Foreshortening is the trick to making Magmortar look like it's really pointing its arm towards you. Things that are closer to you will look larger, and things that are farther away will look smaller. So Magmortar's extended arm is shorter than its other arm, but it will also look bigger!

5 Magmortar will look scorching hot once you color it in shades of bright red, yellows, and soot black. Don't forget some pink for the details, including the spikes on its back.

ELECTIVIRE

Electivire, the evolved form of Electabuzz, packs quite a charge! Watch out for Electivire's two wiry tails—it can use them to touch a target and release over 20,000 volts of power. And thanks to its Motor Drive Ability, Electric-type moves will only pump Electivire up. The more electricity you hit it with, the faster it gets!

Drawing Electivire is a great way to study techniques to make your Pokémon look three-dimensional. All it takes is a few details, like some small lines to show which way Electivire's arms are swinging, or the curved stripes on its body!

1
Once you draw your guidelines, all you need is one big oval for Electivire's body. Add circles for Electivire's hands and ovals for its feet.

2
Does this look like a lot of lines to add at once? All you need to do is take your time! Block in Electivire's legs and extend the circles of Electivire's hands to make its forearms. You'll also want to draw the overlapping plates on Electivire's shoulders before you add in its two tails.

3

Use jagged lines on Electivire's shoulders and the tops of its feet. Then add in Electivire's markings. Look closely at the picture for the little lines on Electivire's elbows—they're actually important to show you which way its arms are pointed!

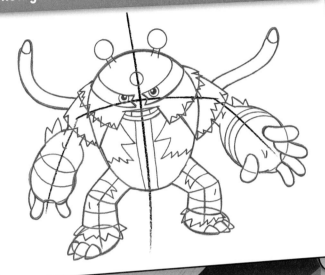

4

Feeling charged up for this last step? Erase your guidelines and see how your Electivire looks!

5

With its bright yellow body and black stripes, Electivire is a walking high voltage warning! Don't forget a vivid red for its gleaming eyes and the tips of its tails.

See how the stripes on Electivire's hands curve in different directions? That's one of the little techniques that shows one hand is closer to the viewer, and the other hand is farther away!

BEINGS FROM THE DEPTHS OF SPACE AND TIME

Dialga and Palkia: these two Legendary Pokémon are almost never seen, but they play an important role in Sinnoh's myths and legends. Here's your chance to study both of them and learn the secret to capturing them—on paper, that is!

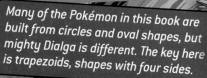

Many of the Pokémon in this book are built from circles and oval shapes, but mighty Dialga is different. The key here is trapezoids, shapes with four sides.

1 First, draw a short, almost horizontal guideline, then the lines for Dialga's neck and each of its front legs. These lines are almost as long as the first guideline. Then block in the shapes for Dialga's head, body, and legs.

2 It's easier to start with the basic shapes here: connect the shapes from Step 1 to outline Dialga's neck and legs. Then add in its tail and the long fin on its head. Once that's done, you're ready for the fin on Dialga's back and the plates on its chest, head, and legs.

DIALGA

Just how old is Dialga? Well, some stories say Dialga appeared at the same moment that time began. Whether the tales are true or not, this Steel-and-Dragon-type Pokémon does have the power to control time. Don't rush when you're drawing Dialga and all of its details— you can take all the time you want!

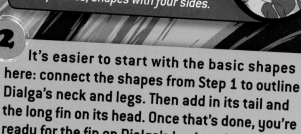

3 That's a lot of details, so take it one at a time. To give its fins and plates a 3D look, draw smaller lines on their ridges. Don't forget the little lines near Dialga's eye! You can even add some short lines near the tops of Dialga's legs to show muscle.

4 Once you erase your guidelines, look over Dialga again to make sure you included all the details.

5 Dialga is shades of cool blue and steely white. Use a darker blue for its body and a light blue for its stripes. Don't forget it has a bright red eye!

Dialga has a special move called the Roar of Time. What does this move look like? Try drawing Dialga in mid-roar!

Step back and look at the blue part of Dialga's body. Underneath its fins and spikes, its basic body shape isn't that complicated after all!

PALKIA

Palkia is another Pokémon featured in the myths of Sinnoh, and the myths say it has power over space. With moves like Spacial Rend, this Water-and-Dragon-type Pokémon definitely has a lot of power! The tales also say that Palkia lives in a parallel dimension gap.

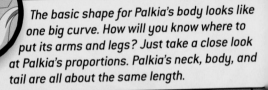

The basic shape for Palkia's body looks like one big curve. How will you know where to put its arms and legs? Just take a close look at Palkia's proportions. Palkia's neck, body, and tail are all about the same length.

1 Draw your guideline and add two shorter guidelines for Palkia's shoulders and legs. Then add a long, curved shape for Palkia's body and the shapes for its shoulders and legs.

2 There are a lot of features to draw at this step, but not to worry! Keep this book in front of you. You won't miss any details if you start with Palkia's head and then work your way down.

3 Now add another layer of details, like Palkia's claws and the other markings on its body. Again, the key is to start at one point, like Palkia's head, and take it from there.

4 Think you've gotten it all? Carefully erase your guidelines and check your drawing.

To add a 3D effect to the pearly orb on Palkia's shoulders, sketch a small circle near the top of the orb. Color this highlight white.

5 Compared to drawing Palkia, coloring it is pretty easy! You'll want to use purple for Palkia's markings, then a light gray for its torso and the inside of its arms.

Dialga weighs twice as much as Palkia does, but Palkia isn't a Pokémon that's easily intimidated. What would happen if Dialga and Palkia were to meet? It's up to you to draw the scene!

1 You'll need several guidelines here. Because it can extend its legs at will, make the guidelines for Darkrai's legs extra long! Then draw an oval resting on top of a semicircular shape. Because Darkrai's head is small, that oval will actually be its torso!

2 Draw Darkrai's head and its near arm first, since they overlap other parts of its body. Fill in the jagged shapes around its waist before you draw in the legs, too. That way, you won't have to erase more lines than necessary.

DARKRAI

Last but certainly not least, it's the ominous Darkrai! Darkrai isn't called the Pitch-Black Pokémon for nothing—it dwells in shadows and has the power to put people and Pokémon to sleep . . . or even give them nightmares! That power comes in useful in battle, along with Darkrai's unique Dark Void move. Sounds grim, doesn't it? But looks aren't always everything, and this Dark-type Pokémon isn't always as sinister as it seems . . .

5 The plume on Darkrai's head is white, its eye is blue, and its collar is red. The rest of Darkrai is black, but it's hard to show details if you color it in with a solid black! Try a dark gray—that way, you can still see all the details you worked so hard on!

3 Now add in more details, including Darkrai's eye. No matter what angle you look at Darkrai from, it only has one eye visible. That makes things easier, doesn't it? Watch out for the little details on Darkrai's arms and neck.

Darkrai can also withdraw its legs and float through the air, too! To draw this form, don't put in lines for Darkrai's legs in Step 1, but follow all the other steps as normal. In Steps 2 and 3, extend Darkrai's "tail" a little bit extra to look like a shadow in the wind!

4 Once you have the details drawn, erase your guidelines and see how your Darkrai is doing.

You've met and drawn some of Sinnoh's mightiest Pokémon, but this is just the beginning! Now that you've mastered these legends, it's time to take on new challenges. Be creative—don't be afraid to experiment with drawing Pokémon in different poses, or even drawing them in their favorite habitat. Whether they're battling, playing, or just relaxing, it's up to you and your imagination. Keep this book handy for reference and practice, and you'll be an expert Pokémon sketch artist in no time!